HIV and Aids

ANDREW CAMPBELL

W
FRANKLIN WATTS
LONDON•SYDNEY

First published in 2004 by Franklin Watts
96 Leonard Street, London EC2A 4XD

Franklin Watts Australia
45-51 Huntley Street
Alexandria, NSW 2015

Copyright © Franklin Watts 2004

Series editor: Rachel Cooke
Series design: White Design
Design: Storeybooks Ltd
Picture research: Diana Morris

Acknowledgements:
David Boe/Corbis: 26. John Cancalosi/Still Pictures: 6. Chalasani/Sipa/Rex
Features: front cover, 11,18. Bob Daemmrich/Image Works/Topham: 23.
Francis Dean/Rex Features: 15. Eskinder Debebe/Rex Features: 5.
Mark Edwards/Still Pictures: 20b, 22. Image Works/Topham: 4,14.
Keystone/Topham: 8t. S Q Lai/Rex Features: 12. Dean Longden/Rex Features: 19.
Richard Lord/Image Works/Topham: 7b. Markus Matzel/Still Pictures: 7t.
Gideon Mendel/Corbis: 27. Shehzad Noorani/Still Pictures: 9.
Picturepoint/Topham: 21. Rex Features: 25. Simon Roberts/Rex Features: 16.
Tony Savino/Image Works/Topham: 29. Sinopix/Rex Features: 28. Sipa/Rex
Features: 8b,13, 24. Friedrick Stark/Still Pictures: 20t. Hjalte Tin/Still Pictures: 10.
Richard Young/Rex Features: 17.

Every attempt has been made to clear copyright. Should there be any inadvertent
omission please apply to the publisher for rectification. The extract in the 'Facing
the Issues' panel on page 27 is taken from the Children's BBC Newsround
website (news.bbc.co.uk/cbbcnews). All figures given are from United Nations
sources (UNAIDS/WHO/UNFPA) unless otherwise stated.

A CIP catalogue record for this book is available from the British Library.

ISBN 0 7496 5786 3

Printed in Belgium

CONTENTS

AIDS IS ONE OF the biggest killers in the world today. Since people became aware of the disease in the early 1980s it has claimed the lives of more than 22 million adults and children. There are other diseases that kill in huge numbers, but none has spread as quickly as Aids in recent times – nor had such an impact on society.

HITTING HARD

Unlike other diseases, which often strike at the very young or the very old, the people most at risk from Aids (Acquired Immune Deficiency Syndrome) are young people and adults in the prime of their lives. This is why many campaigners believe that education is the most important weapon in the battle against Aids and HIV, the virus that leads to the disease (see pages 6–7).

THE POVERTY TRAP

While Aids may not always target the most vulnerable age groups, it certainly targets the most vulnerable parts of the world. Around 95 per cent of people living with HIV and Aids are from developing nations. Poverty is the single biggest reason for this: scientists have invented drugs that help to treat HIV, but many poor countries cannot afford to buy them in large numbers for their citizens.

← Visitors view the Aids memorial quilt in Washington, DC. The quilt was made from over 44,000 individual panels gathered from around the world. Each panel is in memory of a person who has died from Aids.

FOR POORER FOR RICHER

But HIV and Aids are not only a problem for the world's poor. In 2004, HIV infections increased in many developed countries. In the UK, for example, the number of infections rose by 20 per cent for the second year in a row. One worrying trend is the number of young people who think that the disease is no longer a problem. Drugs can help people live with the HIV virus but, for now at least, there is no cure.

AIDS IN THE NEWS

Aids rarely leaves the attention of the world's media, whether because of protests at the lack of access to drugs in the developing world, fears about complacency in the developed world or calls for governments to spend a lot more money to help deal with the crisis. What is often forgotten is the work done by organizations and individuals throughout the world to educate people about the disease and care for those who live with it. For the 40 million people worldwide with HIV and Aids, these efforts offer much-needed hope.

GET THE FACTS STRAIGHT

Reports on Aids often contain statistics about the disease, usually supplied by the United Nations Aids programme (UNAIDS). These statistics are, in fact, estimates, based on HIV rates among pregnant women attending hospitals and clinics in each country. Researchers believe that these rates can show the spread of HIV among the rest of the population, but other people question them. The South African journalist Rian Malan, for example, believes that the real number of people living with HIV and Aids is much lower than the UNAIDS figures. Malan's view is highly controversial, but it highlights the fact that determining HIV and Aids statistics is not a perfect science.

⬇ *A looped ribbon – the symbol of Aids awareness – is illuminated on the UN building in New York during the UN's Special Session on HIV and Aids in 2001.*

A DEADLY VIRUS

HIV STANDS FOR the Human Immunodeficiency Virus. People with the virus are said to be HIV positive. HIV can be caught when certain body fluids – blood, semen and breast milk, among others – come into contact with each other. This can happen in several ways, for example when people have sex without a condom or share needles to inject drugs such as heroin. HIV is not transmitted by kissing or sneezing.

HOW IT WORKS

The HIV virus attacks white blood cells called T-helper cells, which normally protect against diseases. The virus takes over each cell and uses it to make copies of itself, which then infect more T-helper cells. People can be HIV positive for a long time, but if the number of T-helper cells in their body becomes very low they will be unable to fight off other infections, such as pneumonia, or may develop cancer. By this stage, they will have Aids (Acquired Immune Deficiency Syndrome). Aids is the last stage of HIV infection, and can be fatal.

FACING THE ISSUES

Many people believe that humans first caught the HIV virus from chimpanzees. Chimpanzees can carry a similar virus, SIV (Simian Immunodeficiency Virus), which scientists think spread to the human population when someone killed and ate a chimp. While the Aids epidemic did not start until the 1980s, the first infection seems to have happened many years earlier – possibly as far back as the 1930s.

Discussion of the origins of HIV has led some people to blame particular regions of the world for being "the cause" of the virus. But no one can say for certain where the first infection happened – it could have been in Africa, but it could also have been in South America.

← Many people believe the HIV virus originated in chimpanzees.

HELP – AT A PRICE

Drugs called anti-retrovirals (ARVs) can slow the damage the HIV virus causes to the immune system and reduce a person's chance of developing Aids. But people often have to take combinations of many different ARVs, because the HIV virus can quickly become resistant to a single type of treatment. ARVs can also be expensive, and many people in poorer countries cannot afford them (see pages 14–15).

VACCINE HOPES

Scientists are working very hard to produce a vaccine for the HIV virus. One trial in Kenya was set up after the discovery that a number of prostitutes were resistant to HIV – some of their blood cells were able to kill the virus. Scientists have used this information to develop a vaccine, which they began testing in Kenya in 2003. Vaccine trials are slow, however, and take several years to carry out.

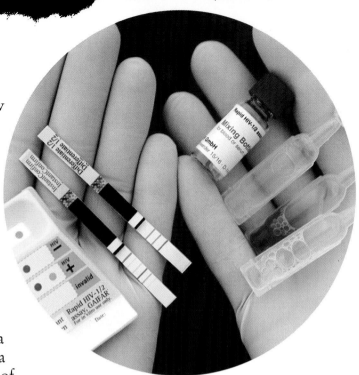

⬆ A selection of different HIV drugs and tests. Treatment with such drugs can be complicated – and costly.

⬇ A doctor examines a volunteer at the Majengo Aids Vaccine Clinic in Nairobi, Kenya. Vaccine trials such as this one offer hope to millions of people.

AIDS IS A RELATIVELY new disease. The first sign of it was a report in June 1981 of a mystery illness that had killed five young gay men in Los Angeles, USA. Rumours spread that only gay people could catch the disease. By 1982, however, doctors noticed the same illness in heterosexual women. Other groups to develop the disease included people who injected drugs and haemophiliacs, whose condition is treated using extracts from other people's blood.

This German poster reads: "A very important resolution for 1988: don't give Aids a chance". In the 1980s, similar poster campaigns appeared across the developed world.

American scientist Dr Robert Gallo, who in 1984 discovered that Aids was caused by the HIV virus.

FEAR AND DOUBT

The early years of the Aids epidemic were a time of great confusion, as no one knew what was causing the disease. Between 1983 and 1984, however, scientists in France and the USA discovered that the cause of Aids was the HIV virus, which could be spread through shared body fluids. Countries such as France, Australia and the UK began high-profile education campaigns to warn people about the risk of infection. Meanwhile, the deaths from Aids of celebrities – such as rock star Freddie Mercury and tennis player Arthur Ashe – reminded people that anyone could get the disease.

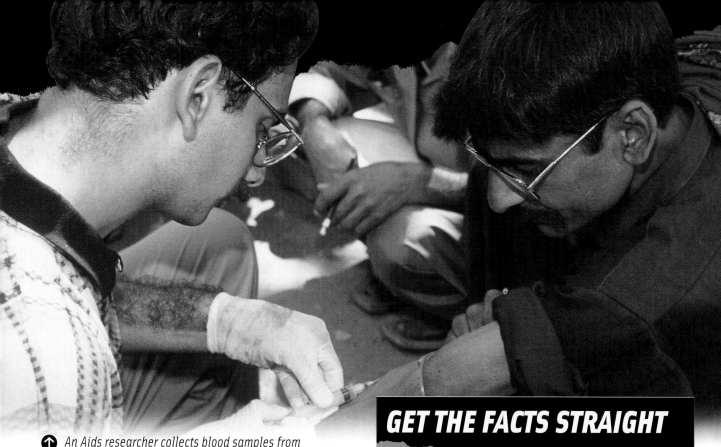

↑ *An Aids researcher collects blood samples from intravenous drug users in Pakistan. Drug users were one of the first groups to contract HIV in large numbers.*

LOOKING AT CAUSES

By 1990, it was estimated that up to 10 million people worldwide had HIV. There were three main factors that had caused the virus to spread so rapidly: the growth in international travel, the increased availability of heroin, and the widespread use of blood transfusions and blood products, such as plasma for haemophiliacs. Before medical staff began screening blood for HIV in 1985, blood transfusions that contained the virus infected many thousands of people.

DIFFERENT STORIES

Aids in the 1990s and 2000s has become a tale of two worlds. In the wealthy developed world, scientific breakthroughs – such as the invention of drugs called protease inhibitors – have massively reduced the number of deaths from Aids and helped people with HIV to live longer, healthier lives. But in the developing world, which often lacks the resources to afford these drugs, the number of people affected by HIV and Aids has continued to grow and grow.

GET THE FACTS STRAIGHT

A short timeline
1981 First Aids cases reported
1982 Aids defined as an illness
1984 HIV identified as the cause of Aids
1985 Screening of blood for HIV begins
1987 The first Aids drug, AZT, launched
1988 First World Aids Day
1991 Basketball player "Magic" Johnson announces he is HIV positive
1994 Tom Hanks wins an Oscar for his role as a gay man with Aids in the film *Philadelphia*
1995 South African president Nelson Mandela speaks out against the stigma that surrounds Aids
1996 Creation of the UN Aids programme (UNAIDS)
1999 Researchers claim that the HIV virus originated in chimpanzees
2002 Launch of the Global Fund to Fight Aids, Tuberculosis and Malaria
2003 US president George W Bush promises $15 billion to fight Aids

AIDS IN AFRICA

IN THE EARLY 1980s, while the developing world was gripped by an Aids panic, Africa became aware of a disease called "slim" – so-called because its victims were often painfully thin. In 1983, cases of slim were confirmed as Aids in Rwanda and Zaire. Aids went on to devastate communities across Africa. In 2003, nearly three-quarters of all the world's people with HIV lived in Africa. More than 15 million Africans have died from Aids.

These children in South Buganda province, Uganda, are raising their hands to indicate that their parents have died from Aids. The impact of Aids on a generation of parents and wage-earners across the continent has been devastating.

WHY AFRICA?

The main reason Aids has had such an impact in Africa is poverty. Africa is the poorest continent in the world, and many people risk infection by trying to make ends meet. Women may be forced to sell sex and men often travel long distances to find work – while away from their homes they may sleep with different partners, some of whom may have HIV. Many African governments are very poor, too, and cannot afford the price of drugs to treat people with HIV and Aids (see pages 14–15).

FACING THE ISSUES

Aids touches nearly everyone's lives in Africa. In 2002, Nelson Mandela, the former South African president, spoke of three members of his family who had died because of the disease. His remarks revealed the silence that still surrounds Aids because of the sense of shame attached to it. "I was aware of the illness of my niece [before she died]," he said, "but I was not aware of the illness of the sons of my nephew until after they had passed away."

DANGEROUS PRACTICES

But other factors have contributed to Africa's Aids epidemic. In the 1990s and 2000s, many African nations struggled with civil wars, which left people very vulnerable. In the 1994 war in Rwanda, tens of thousands of women were infected with HIV after being raped by enemy soldiers. Traditional customs can also spread the disease. In Obwanda, Kenya, women have formed a group to protest against the custom of wife inheritance, when a widow is inherited by her dead husband's brother. The women believe this practice has increased the spread of the HIV virus.

A REASON FOR HOPE

Uganda is one African country that has led the way in responding to the Aids crisis. Unlike other nation's leaders, who were slow to acknowledge the epidemic, Uganda's President Yoweri Museveni put Aids education, prevention and treatment at the top of his country's agenda. The government has funded free handouts of condoms, launched a same-day HIV testing service and sponsored sex education programmes on the radio. These efforts have been rewarded by lower rates of HIV infection, from 15 per cent of the population in 1991 to 6 per cent in 2003.

GET THE FACTS STRAIGHT

Percentage of young people aged 15–24 with HIV in African countries (2001)

Country	Female	Male
Botswana	38%	16%
Zimbabwe	33%	12%
South Africa	26%	11%
Zambia	21%	8%
Kenya	16%	6%
Malawi	15%	6%
Rwanda	11%	5%
Tanzania	8%	4%
Ethiopia	8%	4%
Uganda	5%	2%

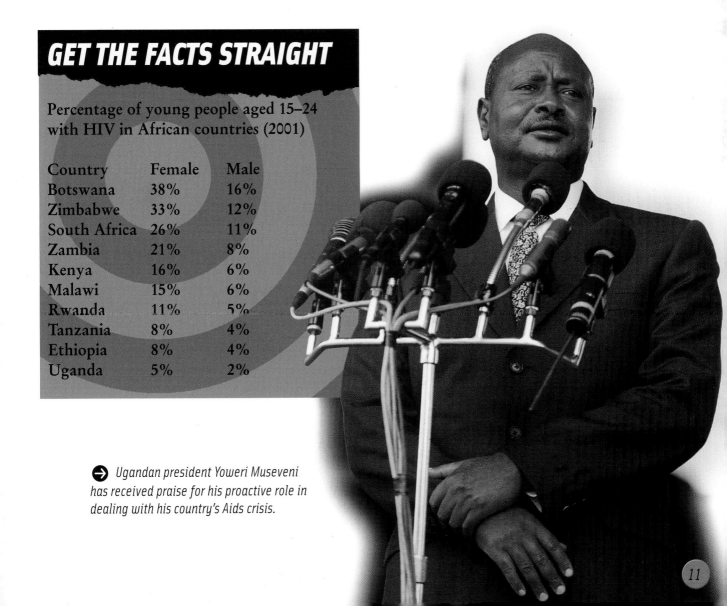

➡ Ugandan president Yoweri Museveni has received praise for his proactive role in dealing with his country's Aids crisis.

THE GLOBAL THREAT

WHILE AIDS HAS CLAIMED more lives in Africa than anywhere else, many other countries have very high levels of infection. In the early 2000s, HIV rates in Eastern Europe, Central Asia, India and China were becoming an increasing cause for concern.

SAME DIFFERENCE

Rises in HIV and Aids rates have the same causes in many parts of the world. They include risky behaviour, such as having unprotected sex and sharing needles, and a lack of education. Other reasons differ from country to country. In China in the early 1990s, up to half a million people were infected by HIV when the government encouraged people to sell their blood to hospitals but failed to ensure the equipment used was properly cleaned.

An Aids sufferer in Henan province, China. Many people contracted HIV in this region as a result of the government's drive to get people to give blood. Blood-collecting equipment was used again and again without being cleaned.

WHAT DO YOU THINK?

Many governments around the world have been accused of not facing up to their Aids epidemics.
- Why do you think some governments are reluctant to accept their Aids problem?
- How would you encourage governments to accept the issue exists?
- What do you think governments need to do to limit the numbers of people with HIV and Aids?

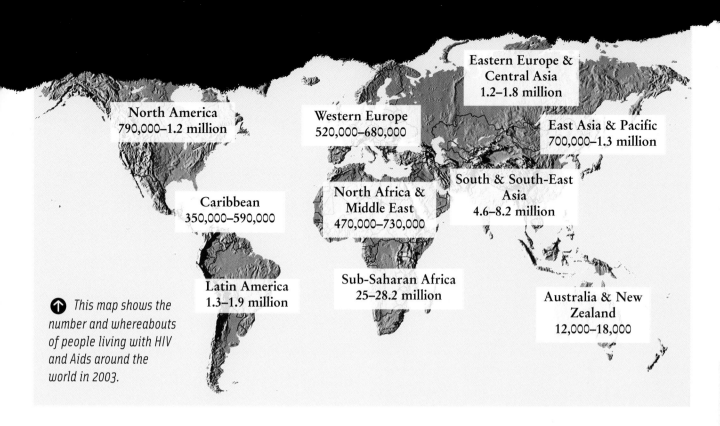

Eastern Europe &
Central Asia
1.2–1.8 million

North America
790,000–1.2 million

Western Europe
520,000–680,000

East Asia & Pacific
700,000–1.3 million

Caribbean
350,000–590,000

North Africa &
Middle East
470,000–730,000

South & South-East
Asia
4.6–8.2 million

Latin America
1.3–1.9 million

Sub-Saharan Africa
25–28.2 million

Australia & New
Zealand
12,000–18,000

⬆ This map shows the number and whereabouts of people living with HIV and Aids around the world in 2003.

A PATTERN OF INFECTION

Unlike Africa, Aids epidemics in other countries are at an earlier stage in their development. The disease spreads in a pattern: the first people to get infected are people in high-risk groups, such as drug users, prostitutes and men who have sex with men. Over time, the virus passes from these groups to the rest of society. From Russia to China, Brazil to India, the highest proportion of cases of HIV and Aids are in these high-risk groups. In Vietnam in 2003, for instance, 65 per cent of HIV infections were among injecting drug users.

FACING UP TO IT

Many people think governments should do more to accept their country's Aids epidemics at this early stage and spend more on treatment and education. India is one country that has been accused of being slow to act. One reason is that Indian people have traditionally not discussed sex in public. But things are changing: the popular Indian TV series *Vijay*, about an HIV positive detective, has a strong theme of Aids awareness.

⬇ Russia's HIV epidemic is affecting different parts of society, including its army.

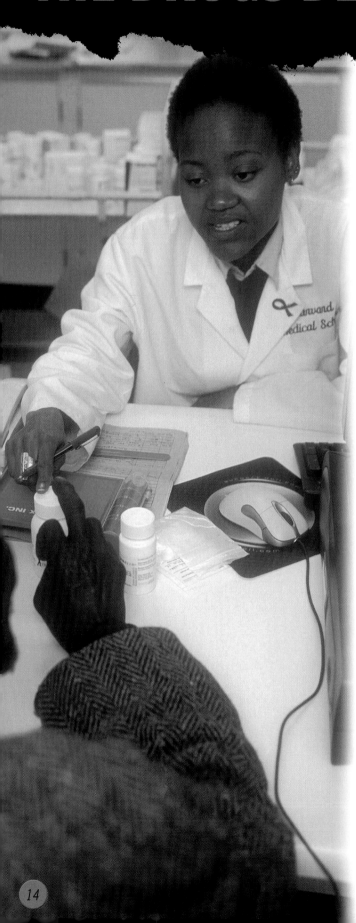

THE BIGGEST PROBLEM with Aids drugs is their expense: treatment can cost more than £6,000 per year. In the developing world, such costs are too much for all but the richest people. Many people campaign for these drugs to be made cheaper – or even free – for the millions of poor people around the world with HIV and Aids.

COPYCATS

In 2000, the Indian drugs company Cipla announced that it would supply poor countries with ARVs (anti-retroviral drugs) for a tenth of the normal price. Cipla is a generic drug company – it produces copies of drugs designed by other manufacturers. Not surprisingly, these other companies oppose generic drugs. They believe that the generics companies are breaking the law, and argue that profits from sales of drugs fund their research. But campaigners for generic drugs argue that anyone who opposes them puts profits before lives.

3 BY 5

The World Health Organization has thrown its weight behind generic drugs. In 2003 it launched its "3 by 5" initiative: to get 3 million people in the developing world on ARVs by 2005. The initiative relies on the use of generic drugs, which people can take as a cocktail of one or two pills, costing as little as £80 a year.

A doctor discusses ARV drugs with a patient in a hospital in Botswana. The patient can only afford the drugs through the support of a charity.

NOT ENOUGH

Many people point out that the cost of generic drugs is still too high – in Malawi, for instance, average wages are £90 a year. ARVs, they argue, should be free. However, even if they were, some people believe very poor countries will not benefit because they lack enough doctors and nurses to administer the drugs. Many health care workers in southern Africa, for example, have gone to work in countries such as the UK, where they can earn better salaries. Some fear that, without proper attention, patients with HIV will not take their medication at the correct times, or may stop altogether, and cause the virus to become resistant to the drugs.

WORKING IT OUT

The French non-governmental organization (NGO) Médecins Sans Frontières (MSF) challenges the view that ARVs cannot work in the developing world, by providing free drugs to people in countries such as Cambodia, Zambia and Kenya. MSF's centre in Kenya uses specially-trained healthcare workers, and not doctors, who offer simple Aids tests and help for people taking their medication.

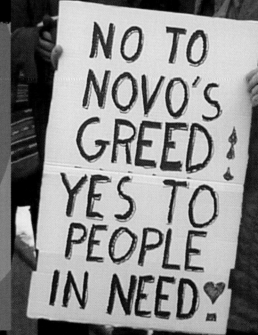

⬇ *A demonstration in Denmark against the drug company Novo Nordic's plans to sue the South African government for allowing the production of generic Aids drugs.*

WHAT DO YOU THINK?

- Do you think drug companies should be allowed to make profits from the sale of medicines for people with HIV and Aids?
- Drug companies argue that they have patents on their products, which protect their inventions. Can you think of any situations when people should be allowed to break these patents?
- Drug companies also argue that it is not their responsibility but that of governments to ensure that people have access to life-saving or life-enhancing treatment. How do you respond to this view?

TOO COMPLACENT?

IN THE 1990s, *the arrival of more effective ARVs meant that deaths from Aids plummeted in the developed world. However, since that time the number of people with HIV in the West has started to rise again. One reason for this is that some people think HIV and Aids are no longer a threat.*

CRISIS? WHAT CRISIS?

In Western Europe in 2002, the number of new HIV cases rose by 23 per cent compared with 2001. Smaller rises also occurred in the USA and Australia. One explanation for the increase is that young people think the epidemic is over. In the words of Gerard, a young Frenchman quoted by *Le Monde* newspaper in 2000: "Aids doesn't interest anyone any more. For the younger generation, Aids is a thing of the past."

⬆ *Clubbers enjoy themselves on the Spanish island of Ibiza. Many young people do not remember the Aids panic of the 1980s – and so may not think they are at risk.*

RISKY BUSINESS

The rise in HIV rates in Western Europe has been driven by a particularly sharp increase in cases in the UK. Here, as in some other countries, there are other reasons apart from complacency for the rise in HIV rates: for example, many new cases are caused by people moving from, or visiting, high-risk regions, such as Africa. But it is hard to judge how large a contribution this is. What is clear is that increases in other sexually transmitted diseases (STDs) among young men and women in many developed countries suggest that more people are having unprotected sex. STDs are more than simply evidence of risky behaviour – they can also make it easier for a person to contract the HIV infection.

IGNORANCE ISN'T BLISS

Many organizations campaign to increase government spending on Aids education, which decreased after the Aids scares of the 1980s and early 1990s. They argue that there is a real need for this education. For example, in 2001 doctors in the USA reported that young people thought a cure for Aids had been found. In 2003, a survey by the UK charity the Terrence Higgins Trust found that nearly two-thirds of young people felt they were not given enough information about the risks of unprotected sex.

⬇ *Pop star Beyoncé Knowles performs at an Aids concert in Cape Town, South Africa, in 2003. Celebrity involvement in Aids campaigns helps to increase young people's awareness about the disease.*

WHAT DO YOU THINK?

In 2001, the Dutch minister of health, Dr Els Borst-Eilers, addressed the United Nations about the danger of complacency about Aids:

"AIDS is a problem of the world. It doesn't know any boundaries. Every country is affected, and the Netherlands has its share in the grievance and loss Aids brings. Since 1985 we have fought a tenacious battle. Our weapons are openness, acknowledgement and information. Involvement of HIV-infected people, intravenous drugs users, homosexuals, sex workers and young people has proven to be key. Infection rates are on the decline for now; however complacency has been deleted from our word-stock. Twenty years after the start of the pandemic, here we are, finally, discussing it at the highest political level – forced to acknowledge that we have fallen short. Twenty years and millions of deaths later, there are no more excuses for denial or anything but openness, decisiveness and leadership."

● Do you think young people are complacent about HIV and Aids?
● If so, what should politicians, teachers, parents and young people themselves do to address the problem?

17

CHILDREN AND AIDS

AIDS AFFECTS MILLIONS *of children around the world in two ways – the children lose parents to the illness or might catch it themselves. Either way, the disease leaves many children facing difficult lives, and can force them into an adult world for which they are not yet prepared.*

CHILDREN AT RISK

Children can become infected with HIV in a number of ways. They might catch the virus from their mothers, either before birth or through breast milk. They might be sexually abused by adults, and catch the virus as a result.

Or they might have unprotected sex or inject drugs without knowing the risks involved. In the Dominican Republic in the Caribbean, for example, young people often experiment with sex at an early age. According to one national report, more than 50 per cent of cases of HIV and Aids in the country are among 12- to 15-year-olds.

AIDS ORPHANS

Coping with HIV or Aids is hard for any child, but so too is losing parents to the disease. In 2003, around 15 million children worldwide had lost one or both parents to Aids, including 11 million in Africa and 2 million in Asia. In some countries the problem isn't restricted to parents: many children have lost aunts, uncles, grandparents and teachers to Aids.

⊗ *Justine sits with her mother, who has Aids, in a hospital in Kampala, Uganda. She will shortly become another Aids orphan.*

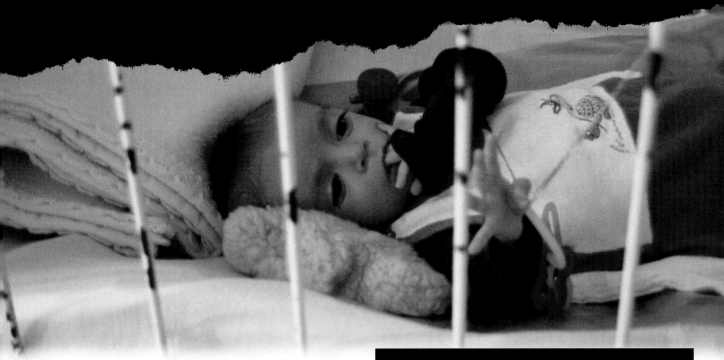

↑ *This baby was one of many thousands in Romania who contracted HIV in the 1980s and early 1990s, the result of contaminated blood transfusions.*

GROWING UP TOO FAST

For poor families, the death of a parent can force a child into new, harsh roles. To help earn money, boys are often made to work on farms or in factories, while girls may be forced into early marriages or prostitution. When both parents have died, a child may have to become the head of the household. This was the situation facing 13-year-old Christopher, from Kassana in Uganda, when the deaths of his mother and father from Aids left him to care for his 9-year-old brother Habatt. One of Christopher's tough choices is whether to go to school or not: if he does, then he worries that there is no one to protect his house and land.

HELPING HANDS

Many organizations are doing all they can to reduce the number of children with HIV and Aids and ease the burden on Aids orphans. In some developing countries, NGOs and drug companies provide free drugs to pregnant women with HIV, which can halve the risk of their babies catching the virus. Other NGOs

FACING THE ISSUES

In the late 1980s, thousands of children in Romania became infected with HIV. Many of the children were orphans and, because food and vitamins were in short supply, doctors gave them small transfusions of blood. Unfortunately, this blood was contaminated. Today, these children receive full drug treatment from the government. They continue to face many problems, but some, such as 14-year-old Ciprian, are optimistic about the future. He told the *New York Times* newspaper about his ambition to become a carpenter and build his own house, get married and set up a business to help street children.

provide children with financial and emotional support. One scheme that has become popular across Africa is for parents dying of Aids to write "memory books" for their children. The books help children to remember their families, but also record any property their parents have left them – which can help stop other people claiming it.

WOMEN AND AIDS

WOMEN PLAY A VITAL ROLE in any strategy for dealing with HIV and Aids. This is because in some countries women – especially young women – are more likely to catch the virus than men. But it is also because women in long-term relationships can be the link through which the disease passes from high-risk groups to the rest of society.

HIGH RISK GROUP

The total number of people with HIV and Aids includes slightly more men than women. However, in 2001, 62 per cent of 15- to 24-year-olds with HIV were female. There are several reasons why young women are more at risk. The first is physical – it is easier for a woman to catch the virus.

⬆ A poster in Johannesburg, South Africa, stresses the role women play in dealing with HIV and Aids. Many argue this role is hampered by male attitudes.

OUT OF CONTROL

Economic and cultural factors also contribute to the problem. Many women depend on men financially and have no control over when they have sex, or may have to work as prostitutes to support themselves. Different cultures' expectations can also increase the risk to women. For example, some societies accept that women should marry older, sexually-experienced men.

⬅ A volunteer hands out condoms to a prostitute in Bangkok, Thailand. Prostitutes face a constant risk of HIV infection.

FAMILIAR STORIES

Another practice accepted in many societies is for men to sleep with a number of different partners, including prostitutes, as well as their wives or girlfriends. If the men catch HIV, their wives or girlfriends will probably catch it, too. The story of Madavi, who lives in Chennai, India, is similar to those of thousands of other women around the world. Madavi was infected with HIV by her husband, a truck driver who slept with other women when he was away from home. As a result, three of her five children were born HIV positive.

TOO UNEQUAL

One big problem is the lack of equality between women and men. For example, men sometimes ignore women's requests for them to use condoms. And if a women's husband dies from Aids and she herself has the illness, she might have to keep quiet in the hope of finding a new husband who can provide for her. In 2004, the United Nations Aids programme (UNAIDS) acknowledged this problem when it launched the Global Coalition on Women and Aids. The Coalition aims to prevent new HIV infections among women and girls, to promote equal access to treatment and to protect a woman's right to inherit her husband's property if he dies.

FACING THE ISSUES

One HIV positive woman who teaches others about the risks of HIV is Princess Kasune Zulu. In her native Zambia, Princess (her first name, not a title) has hosted a radio phone-in programme called *Positive Living*. She also educates truck drivers about the dangers of sleeping with different women on their journeys – and the risk this behaviour poses for their partners back home. Princess believes that women need more knowledge and equal treatment to combat Aids: "Changing the lot of women is the key to turning things around. Not enough women are empowered. Not enough of them are educated about Aids and not enough of them have their own home or a job which would help them assert themselves."

➔ A newly-married couple in India. Many married women feel unable to ask their husbands to wear condoms and not to sleep with other women.

AIDS HAS NO CURE

CONDOMISE AND STAY ALIVE!!

MANY PEOPLE SEE *education as the real hope in the fight against Aids, both for children before they become sexually active and for young people and adults who live with the risk of contracting the disease.*

NEVER TOO EARLY

The 5- to 15-year-old age group in Africa is regarded as the "generation of hope" since they have the lowest rates of HIV infection and there is still time to teach them how to protect themselves against the disease. Young children learn about Aids through songs and storytelling, while, with older children, teachers openly discuss issues such as condom use.

Children play with their teacher in Francistown, Botswana, in front of Aids posters. The posters reinforce the information about Aids the children are receiving through song and dance.

STREET LIFE

But education is important outside the classroom, too – especially for young people and adults who may not know all the facts about HIV and Aids. Street education is one way to get the message across to those people who have left school or never attended it in the first place. One initiative of this kind has been set up in Addis Ababa, Ethiopia, where a group of actors regularly perform songs and short plays that teach the audience about the disease.

MODEL EXAMPLE

Another way is to teach by example. Médecins Sans Frontières flew two HIV positive models from the USA to the Democratic Republic of Congo. The male models showed people how to take ARV drugs, and their own healthy appearances demonstrated the benefits of staying on the medication.

PEER PRESSURE

Another form of education is peer education, which involves people teaching other people in their same social group. Peer education among young people has become popular throughout Latin America, especially in countries such as Ecuador, where the school curriculum does not cover HIV prevention. Peer education can be used in a range of settings. For example, in Vietnam hairdressers are trained to offer advice to prostitutes who come for a haircut.

↘ *Students in Texas discuss health issues. Peer education can be a powerful way of increasing awareness about Aids.*

MEDIA MESSAGES

Governments in the developed world are also realising that the need for Aids teaching has not gone away – something that rising levels of HIV and other STDs demonstrates (see pages 16–17). But the media also has a role to play. One example is the "Staying Alive" campaign launched by MTV. Through television shows, a website and posters, the campaign aims to inform young people in the developed and the developing world about HIV and Aids.

GET THE FACTS STRAIGHT

Here are some of the different types of Aids education:

- ● Classroom teaching
- ● Street education
- ● Peer education
- ● Advice and counselling
- ● Radio and television programmes
- ● Poster campaigns and leaflets
- ● Telephone helplines
- ● Websites

IN 2001 KOFI ANNAN, *the United Nation's Secretary-General, called on governments around the world to give $10 billion a year towards solving the global Aids crisis. In 2003, however, governments gave only a third of this amount and large donations are rarely straightforward: governments expect to have a say about where and on what their money is spent.*

LOWERING EXPECTATIONS

Kofi Annan called for the $10-billion-a-year funding at the launch of the Global Fund to Fight Aids, Tuberculosis and Malaria – an international programme to coordinate donations and spending on HIV prevention and treatment. But the limited resources of the Global Fund mean that some countries desperately in need of help have been disappointed. Malawi, for example, asked the Global Fund for money to put 300,000 people on ARV drugs. It had to reduce this number to 50,000 people.

Demonstrators in Paris, in 2003, demand that governments give more money to the Global Aids Fund.

DIFFERENT PRIORITIES

There are a variety of reasons why the Global Fund has received less money than the United Nations hoped for. One is that the terrorist attacks on the USA on 11 September 2001 have made fighting terrorism a higher priority for some countries than fighting Aids. Another reason is that governments would rather spend money on Aids programmes they themselves control, rather than give it to an international organization, such as the Global Fund, to spend on their behalf.

STRINGS ATTACHED?

The USA is one country that prefers to control how its donations are spent. In 2003, its president, George W Bush, delighted campaigners when he promised $15 billion to fight Aids. But this money will not necessarily be available to all Aids programmes. The US Congress, for example, has demanded that 10 per cent of the money goes on education programmes that promote abstinence (not having sex) rather than condom use, even though some people argue that, because of their lack of equality, women can find abstinence very difficult to achieve.

US president George W Bush, during his 2003 speech that announced $15 billion funding to help deal with HIV and Aids. Some people are nervous that much of this money will only go to projects that agree with views held by conservative American politicians.

WHAT DO YOU THINK?

- Kofi Annan has described Aids as "the real weapon of mass destruction". Do you think governments should spend as much on Aids as they do on war and fighting terrorism?
- What advantages and disadvantages can you think of for programmes that promote abstinence and programmes that promote condom use?
- How would you persuade a government to give more to the Global Fund to Fight Aids, Tuberculosis and Malaria?
- Do you think it is fair that a government should have a say in how any donation it made to the Global Fund was spent?

THE STIGMA OF HIV AND AIDS has been described as one of the worst aspects of the disease. It can stop people coming forward for testing and treatment, and can put their jobs, homes and even lives at risk. People with HIV and Aids have rights just like anyone else – including the right to be protected from discrimination.

EXCLUSION AND WORSE

Sometimes discrimination excludes people from the rest of society. In Kerala, India, in 2003, two children were banned from their school and refused access to other schools because they were HIV positive. Sometimes discrimination leads to death. In South Africa in 1998, the Aids campaigner Gugu Dlamini was beaten to death by her neighbours after publicly declaring that she was HIV positive.

TAKING LIBERTIES

Besides exclusion and violence, discrimination can take the form of acting without a person's consent. Such actions include testing people – for instance prisoners or refugees – for HIV and revealing to others if a person is HIV positive. In Thailand, 40 per cent of people who answered a UNAIDS survey said that their HIV positive status had been revealed to someone else without their permission.

← In 1985, Ryan White, a haemophiliac with Aids, was banned from his school in Indiana, USA. He became a symbol of Aids discrimination.

THE SHAME EFFECT

The more people experience or hear about discrimination, the more they can feel ashamed. The results can be deadly: people may decide against being tested for HIV or may not insist that their partner uses a condom, in case it looks as if they already have the disease. In developing countries that offer free ARVs to HIV positive pregnant women, many expecting mothers do not come for treatment, for fear of revealing their illness.

POSITIVE EXAMPLES

But efforts are being made around the world to tackle discrimination and uphold people's rights. In Brazil, for example, the Volkswagen company has introduced measures that guarantee the right to confidentiality of workers who have HIV or Aids. And in South Africa, the murder of Gugu Dlamini led one campaigning group to produce T-shirts with the words "HIV POSITIVE" in large letters. The T-shirts were worn by many people – including the then president, Nelson Mandela.

➡ *A member of South Africa's Treatment Action Campaign wears a "HIV positive" T-shirt – first produced in response to the murder of Gugu Dlamini.*

FACING THE ISSUES

People with HIV and Aids face discrimination whatever their age and wherever they live. Lynn, a teenager from London, UK, reveals her experience living with HIV:

"I was diagnosed HIV positive at the age of eight... It's hard trying to live and cope with as normal a life as possible. The thing that hurts the most is the fact that some of my school friends can talk openly when they're ill and no one would joke about it or say anything nasty. But when it comes to HIV and Aids you just have to keep quiet. Many young people like myself have to live a life based around this secret because there is a lot of ignorance and prejudice towards HIV/Aids sufferers. The thing that keeps me going is having a lot of people there to support me. Talking to other young people who are in the same situation as me really helps to inspire and give me the courage to keep going and to enjoy life."

H.I.V. POSITIVE

ISSUED BY TREATMENT ACTION CAMPAIGN PROJECT ULWAZI FOR SCHOOLS AIDS WEEK

↑ *A crowded street in Shanghai, China. Many people fear that the Aids crisis in China – which has one fifth of the world's population – is only just beginning.*

IN 2003, 40 MILLION people worldwide lived with HIV and Aids. By 2010, the World Health Organization (WHO) predicts this figure will be 87 million. The Aids crisis rests on a knife-edge: on the one hand is the prospect of more and more people becoming infected; on the other the hopes of a vaccine, more access to drugs, and an even stronger effort to make sure everyone knows the dangers of catching HIV – and how to protect themselves.

WORST-CASE SCENARIO

Another grim prediction is that the global Aids epidemic is not likely to peak until the middle of the 21st century – in other words, things are going to get worse before they can get better. Experts fear that countries such as India, China and Russia may all develop Aids epidemics on a similar scale to Africa's – there are already large numbers of HIV infections among these nations' high-risk groups (see pages 12–13).

SOCIAL CHANGE?

Some people believe that the only way to tackle the Aids crisis is to address deep-rooted problems, such as the income gap between the world's poorest and richest countries and the inequality that exists between men and women in many societies. Others argue that this sort of change could take years to achieve; in the meantime, the only way to prevent more people becoming infected is through education.

TESTING TIMES

For many, science offers the best hope of beating the disease. Scientists are currently researching a number of possible vaccines for the HIV virus – including one made from monkey protein and one which is based on the vaccine for smallpox, a highly infectious disease that was eradicated from the world in 1979. Scientists have already done much to make ARV drugs simpler to take, but the hope is that soon they will be simpler still and have less unpleasant side effects.

MORE – PLEASE

From global initiatives organized by UNAIDS and WHO to thousands of national and local projects set up by NGOs and individuals, much is being done to prevent the spread of Aids, treat people who have the disease and deal with discrimination. To ensure that the worst predictions do not happen many campaigners, politicians and – above all – those who live with HIV and Aids agree that much more needs to be done.

WHAT DO YOU THINK?

Here are some of the demands that campaigners argue governments and businesses must meet to solve the world's Aids crisis:

- Drug companies should lower their prices for ARVs
- Generic drug companies should be allowed to make cheap copies of drugs for poor countries
- Governments should give the Global Fund to Fight Aids, Tuberculosis and Malaria the $10 billion a year requested by the United Nations
- Rich countries should stop recruiting doctors and nurses from poorer nations
- Rich countries should write off any debts they are owed by poor nations
- All governments should spend more on Aids education in their own countries

Do you agree with all of these demands? Are there any you disagree with? Why? What other demands would you make to deal with the Aids crisis?

An Aids researcher at work in a laboratory. Aids treatments have advanced a great deal since the 1980s – but more research is vital.

GLOSSARY

Aids (Acquired Immune Deficiency Syndrome): A collection of infections and cancers that people with HIV can develop.

ARV (anti-retroviral): A drug that acts against the HIV virus by stopping it making copies of itself inside T-helper cells.

blood transfusion: Taking blood from one or many donors and giving it to someone who needs it for medical reasons.

developed world: A term for countries with high levels of industry, technology and personal wealth, as well as stable health care systems.

developing world: A term for generally poor countries that have low levels of industry and technology and in which many people work in farming.

discrimination: Unfair treatment of people because of who they are, for example because they have HIV or Aids.

epidemic: A situation when a lot of people in one area are infected with the same disease.

generic drug: A drug that is a copy of another one. With no research and development costs, generic drugs are often cheap.

haemophiliac: Someone with a condition that means their blood cannot clot properly, so even a small cut can cause them to lose lots of blood. Haemophiliacs use a substance from other people's blood to allow their blood to clot.

HIV (Human Immunodeficiency Virus): The virus that causes people to develop Aids. Once someone is infected with HIV it stays with them for life.

immune system: The body's defence system against disease-carrying micro-organisms.

intravenous drug use: Using a needle to inject drugs, like heroin, directly into the bloodstream.

NGO (Non-Governmental Organization): An independent, not-for-profit organization that campaigns, provides a service or helps people.

resistance: When a virus alters itself and becomes less sensitive to a drug treatment.

rights: Claims to freedom, equal treatment and resources that are guaranteed in law.

STDs (Sexually Transmitted Diseases): Diseases that are caught through sexual contact.

side effects: Unwanted additional effects from taking a drug.

stigma: A sense of shame – in the case of HIV and Aids, usually because of discrimination.

T-helper cell: A type of white blood cell that helps defend the body against infections.

United Nations: The international organization established in 1945 to promote peace and cooperation between countries.

UNAIDS (Joint United Nations Programme on HIV/Aids): An agency of the United Nations, created in 1996 to lead the world's response to the Aids crisis.

vaccine: A treatment that uses micro-organisms to stimulate the body's defences so it can fight off an infection.

virus: A micro-organism that uses the living cells of an animal or plant to reproduce.

WHO (World Health Organization): An agency of the United Nations, established in 1948 to promote health and tackle disease around the world.

WORLD ORGANIZATIONS

Family Health International (FHI)

www.fhi.org

FHI is an international public health organization. Its website contains profiles of the HIV situation in different countries and "YouthNet", a section for young people about HIV and Aids.

The Global Fund to Fight Aids, Tuberculosis and Malaria

www.theglobalfund.org

Find out about the projects the Global Fund is sponsoring all over the world.

United Nations Aids programme (UNAIDS)

www.unaids.org

Find out more about UNAIDS and read the country-by-country information as well as the organization's annual report, Aids Epidemic Update.

UNICEF

www.unicef.org/aids/index.html

UNICEF is the United Nations Children's Fund, which aims to improve children's lives all over the world. This part of its website discusses how Aids affects children, providing real-life examples from all over the world.

World Health Organization

www.who.int

WHO's website has a huge amount of information about every type of disease, including lots on HIV and Aids. Find out more about its "3 by 5" campaign to provide Aids drugs to 3 million people in the developing world.

NON-GOVERNMENTAL ORGANIZATIONS

Action Aid

www.actionaid.org

This NGO works to fight poverty worldwide, so the HIV and Aids section of its website has lots on the links between the disease and poverty. The "Action Zone" webpages contain ideas on how you can help tackle the problems of HIV and Aids.

Avert

www.avert.org

Avert is an international Aids charity. This excellent site contains statistics, the history of HIV and Aids, questions and answers, personal stories and much more.

Global Aids Alliance

www.globalaidsalliance.org

The website of a US-based NGO that campaigns to stop the worldwide Aids epidemic. Read about the action it takes to make governments aware of the problems.

Médecins Sans Frontières

www.msf.org

Find out about the work of this medical NGO, which is actively involved in the treatment of people with HIV and Aids in the developing world.

Terrence Higgins Trust

www.tht.org.uk

The Terrence Higgins Trust is the oldest and largest Aids charity in Europe, established in 1982. Its website has lots of information about HIV, Aids and safe sex.

MEDIA AND INFORMATION SITES

Like It Is

www.likeitis.org

A website for young people, which discusses relationships, sex, puberty, STDs and other topics in a clear and open way.

Staying Alive

www.staying-alive.org

The website of MTV's "Staying Alive" Aids awareness campaign contains clearly presented facts about the disease, as well as clips of famous musicians singing at Aids concerts and discussing the crisis.

INDEX